To: Millie

From: Lori, Carol, Dolly and
all the McAuliffe Family

We wish you peace of mind,
heart and spirit as you
remember, always, your
beloved husband, John.

You are thought of in a special way...

A SONG OF REMEMBRANCE

Light a Candle

PAUL ALEXANDER

PAUL ALEXANDER'S BEREAVEMENT AND MUSIC RESOURCES AVAILABLE AT GRIEFSONG.COM
OR CALL 800.538.4158

PUBLISHED BY PAUL ALEXANDER, P.O. BOX 858 AMAGANSETT, N.Y 11930

IMAGES AND PHOTOGRAPHS PROVIDED BY INDEXOPEN, SUPERSTOCK, STOCKBYTE,
DYNAMIC GRAPHICS, AND MARY ELLEN FATA.

ISBN: 0-9642-0832-6

PRINTED IN CHINA

Light a Candle

And I will light a candle for you
To shatter all the darkness and bless the times we knew.
Like a beacon in the night
The flame will burn bright and guide us on our way.
Oh, today I light a candle for you.

The seasons come and go, and I'm weary from the change.
I keep on moving on, you know it's not the same.
And when I'm walking all alone, do you hear me call your name?
Do you hear me sing the songs we used to sing?

You filled my life with wonder, touched me with surprise,
I always saw that something special deep within your eyes.
And through the good times and the bad, we carried on with pride.
I hold on to the love and life we knew.
Oh, today I light a candle for you.

Rituals are powerful, symbolic actions.

They enable the bereaved to express grief in visible form and movement. Lighting a candle, planting a tree, releasing a balloon, walking a special path create moments of connection to our loved ones. When joined with others in these meaningful events, we create opportunities for healing and unite in a community and family of support.

LIGHT A CANDLE is a song which sings of the power of the relationship and the connection shared. The memories and the living essence of your loved one are etched in your heart, soul and mind. They are forever yours.

Before you listen to the gift of song within this book, light a candle for your loved one. Let the glow of the flame and sound of the music fill the empty spaces of your heart and home with a gentle reminder of your loved one's presence and spirit. Their light forever shines. May it guide your steps and comfort the hurting and lonely places.

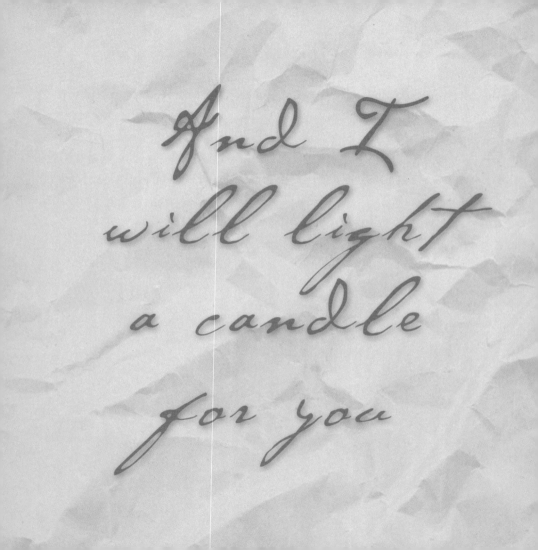

to shatter all

the darkness

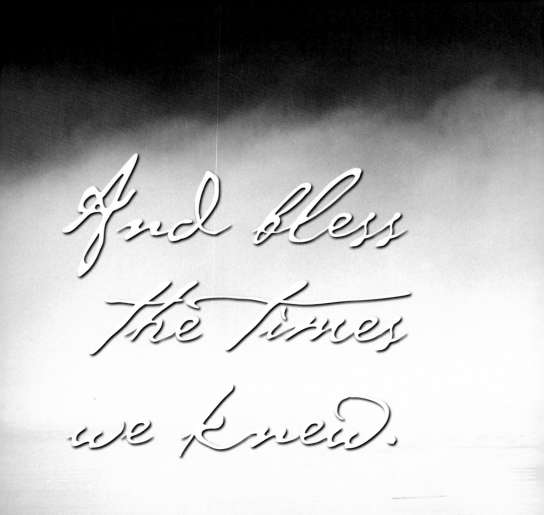

And bless
the Times
we knew.

As we lit the candles for my mother's eightieth birthday celebration I asked her some words of advice. She smiled and said "To thine own self be true."

How can we be true to ourselves as we face our grief and losses? I cannot walk your path, nor you walk mine. Know your truth and honor it in words and action with compassion and grace.

If you are ever struggling with a decision or direction in your life, quiet your mind in prayer or meditation and imagine yourself talking with your loved one. What would they say or how would they advise you? Love never dies. They are a thought away.

The flame

will burn
bright

and guide us on our way

Oh, today
I light
a candle
for you.

The seasons come and go,

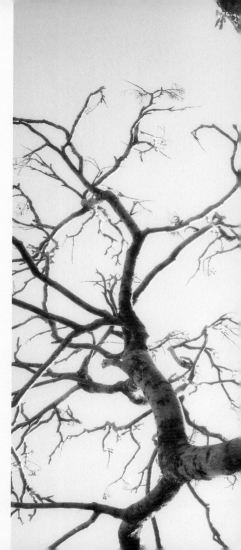

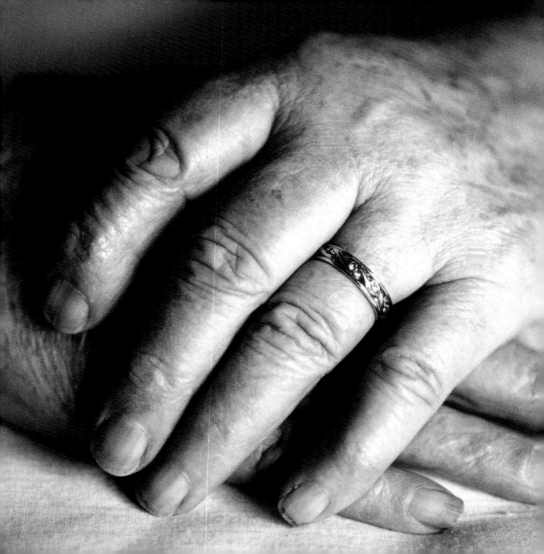

And I'm
weary
from the
change.

I KEEP
ON
MOVING
ON

i keep on moving on

I KEEP ON MOVING O

you know
its not
the same.

We all have favorite stories of our loved one.

Share your story with others.

Cherish each memory and ask others
to share their favorite stories with you.

Write these memories in a journal or
ask for letters from your family and friends.

In the quiet moments take time to see how
the life of your loved one made a difference
to you and to others.

Create a treasure chest of hope and memory.

and when
I'm walking
all alone

Do you hear me
call your name?

Do you hear me
sing the songs
we used to sing?

YOU filled
my LIFE
with
WONDER

Touched me
with
SURPRISE

I always said
that something
special
deep within
your eyes

Thank you for
the gift...

Why do certain people come into our lives?

Those who love us and whom we love are the stuff
upon which life is made. All relationships have
a certain hue and significance all their own.

How did your loved one touch your life?

What was it that they loved most about you?

What qualities did they encourage and bring out in you
that you can still bring to the world around you.
It is not always the matter of how long you shared and loved,
but that you loved and were loved.

What is the gift and the purpose of this special bond?

Some gifts come wrapped in fancy paper and ribbons
and others come in the quiet stirring of the heart.

There is a purpose and a meaning to the time
and love you shared.

We carried on with PRIDE.

I hold on to
the love
and life
we knew.

Oh, today
I light
a candle
for you.